WITH THIS NIGHT

Binah Yitzrit Foundation Series in Israel Studies

WITH THIS NIGHT

LEAH GOLDBERG

TRANSLATED FROM THE HEBREW
AND INTRODUCED BY ANNIE KANTAR

The Center for Middle Eastern Studies
The University of Texas at Austin

Library of Congress Control Number: 2011923968
ISBN: 978-0-292-72647-5

Originally published in Hebrew by Sifriat Poalim.

This book was made possible by generous support from the Binah Yitzrit Foundation.

For Yotam

—*Annie Kantar*

CONTENTS

ACKNOWLEDGMENTS

Grateful acknowledgment is extended to the editors of *New Translations, Poetry International, Smartish Pace,* and *Tikkun,* where several of these translations first appeared in earlier versions.

This work owes its existence to many people. I'd like to thank the Fulbright Program, Dr. Karen Alkalay-Gut, and the Department of English at Tel Aviv University, for affording me the time to immerse myself in Hebrew literature. For their kindness, guidance, and wisdom over the years, I am deeply grateful to Michael Collier, Phillis Levin, Shara McCallum, and Stanley Plumly. Conversations with Harry Aveling, Nati Brooks, Joy Ladin, Christine Perrin, and many other friends have enriched this manuscript at various stages. My heartfelt thanks for their advice, poetic and otherwise. Profound gratitude is extended to Peter Cole, for gently and patiently having shown me the questions I've needed to ask while working with Goldberg's poems. I am deeply indebted to Giddon Ticotsky, whose abundance of spirit and scholarship has informed these translations on occasions too many to count. My thanks to the Center for Middle Eastern Studies at the University of Texas and especially my editor, Wendy Moore, for the dexterity and care with which they have handled every aspect of publication. Thank you to my family (on both sides of the sea) for their encouragement of this work, and especially to my parents. And finally, thank you to Yotam, with whom those things that I most cherish in Goldberg come alive.

TRANSLATOR'S NOTE

"A poet finds corresponding sounds in language the way a sculptor finds Venus in a block of marble," wrote Leah Goldberg in one of her essays on literature, and her poems embody this essential tension between deliberation and inevitability. On the one hand, the reader registers the careful chiseling of lines and stanzas; on the other, she feels that, somehow, sound and sense were correlated all along in a unity that needed only to be revealed.

How the best words—or in Goldberg's case, the best sounds—seem to fall effortlessly into their best order is anyone's guess, though her journals and correspondence suggest that her poems were the product of a singular talent put through rigorous paces over a period of many years. Among her most widely recognized achievements is the delicate yet sonorous music of her poems. In this final collection published during her lifetime, Goldberg stretched and recast inherited formal structures in favor of a more supple and sinuous line, yet the lyric integrity of her verse remained intact as ever. Rather than seek to achieve one-for-one equivalence with Goldberg's prosodic strategies, I've aimed to replicate the *effects* of those strategies. Therefore, full rhyme sometimes yields to half rhyme and assonance, end rhyme to internal rhyme, and meter to a similar, though not identical, pattern of stress and emphasis. In the same spirit, I have held close to the poems' phrase-by-phrase meanings with attention to their musical, tonal, and cultural resonances. By and large, I've avoided paraphrase, and any instances of divergence have been indicated in the endnotes. Above all, I have tried to approach these translations with the "modesty, surrender, and care" that Goldberg deemed essential when working with poetic form.

Capturing the imaginative spell of a poem is largely a matter of lying low and letting the poems make themselves known, often more slowly than one would like. This receptivity may actually be the most difficult step in the translation process—though it has been essential amid the drafts, deletions, and revisions that have amassed in the wake of these translations. I hope that in some small measure, the experience of reading Goldberg—that particular sense of wholeness that was hers alone—might be felt and found in these pages.

Jerusalem
December 2010

INTRODUCTION

I went home quite happy. And it was so good to walk all alone, not to talk to anyone, and even when nearly all the people walked in a different direction . . . Sometimes, I feel that here, I truly am—myself. Only I don't know where I am.[1]

Perhaps she was capable of finding herself only in foreignness. Surely she knew by the fall of 1960, when she wrote these lines in her journal while in Copenhagen, that she would never know exactly where she belonged. The author of nine collections of poetry, three plays, a memoir, three novels, dozens of children's books, and hundreds of literary essays and commentary; translator of Ibsen, Tolstoy, Petrarch, Shakespeare, and others; and a mentor to then-emerging poets such as Dan Pagis and Dahlia Ravikovitch, Goldberg used the journal—an otherwise blank student exam booklet from the Hebrew University of Jerusalem, where she founded the Department of Comparative Literature—for jotting down thoughts on paintings she saw in museums, operas she attended, visits with acquaintances she avoided, and drafting "Journey Without a Name," one of the poems of what would turn out to be the final collection she published in her lifetime, *With This Night*.

A writer whose allegiances traversed genres and continents, who drew readers, students, and friends of all stripes, Goldberg frequently struggled with an almost existential sense of namelessness. Today, mention of her name will evoke a nostalgic sigh among Israelis who have grown up hearing her poems read, quoted, recollected, and—having been set to some four hundred melodies—sung on the radio. Her collection of selected poems,

Early and Late, which first appeared in 1959, remains one of the best-selling books of poetry ever published in Israel. Her work as a translator from multiple languages made her an ambassador of sorts, bringing Western European culture to the Hebrew literary landscape. And her passionate lectures on literature, as well as the columns she wrote in the daily newspapers, expanded her impact on Israeli cultural life. In 1970, as the committee that was to grant Israel's most prestigious award of artistic achievement, the Israel Prize, was convening, Goldberg passed away. The committee awarded her the prize posthumously.

"More geography than biography"[2] is the way that Goldberg described, with characteristic matter-of-factness, her peripatetic childhood. In a certain sense, her assessment may be applied to her life as a whole. Even the occasion of her approaching birth (May 29, 1911) sent her family packing, leaving their home in Kovno (now Kaunas), Lithuania, for a brief visit to Königsberg (now Kaliningrad, Russia), where they hoped to find more modern hospital facilities than those in their hometown. Four years later, shortly after the outbreak of World War I, the Jewish population of Kovno was ordered to leave, and Goldberg's family, together with some one hundred twenty thousand Jews, was sent into exile. Over the next three years as she and her family wandered through "cold and hunger," the young Goldberg subsisted on black bread, a smattering of local friends, and tales she conjured about an elusive skirt that ventured from place to place.[3]

"I'm from there— / the village of small winds,"[4] Goldberg would write decades later, in one of the few poems where she recalls her childhood Kovno. Upon her family's return from exile, she gained acceptance into the Russian trade school; within months it was transformed into a Hebrew gymnasium, and the language of study changed in turn. One of many grassroots

Zionist schools of its kind that sprang up in Europe and the former Soviet Union, it was here that she acquired the basis of her Hebrew (together with the five other languages that were part of the curriculum), and by her early teenage years, she was writing her poems in Hebrew alone. Fully foreign, and at the same time more her own than her native Russian would ever be, Hebrew was both a fateful outcome of her education as well as a deliberate choice for this ambitious Jewish girl who held a common dream of the time—of one day living in Palestine. "One chooses a language," Goldberg would write of her adopted mother tongue, "the way one chooses a ring."[5] Later, weighing in on the linguistic proclivities of her generation, she explained: "Because Hebrew was, for us, a matter of choice and not a natural offshoot of our lives, I choose it to this day, each day, moment by moment, anew."[6]

Though Goldberg would occasionally wax nostalgic over the proverbial lost land of her childhood, had she been forced to stay in Kovno, she reflected later in an interview, she was sure that she "would have rather not lived."[7] Released from her hometown at the age of nineteen with a scholarship to the Universities of Berlin and Bonn, there—in the heart of Western Europe in the late 1920s and early 1930s—the young Goldberg was finally able to dwell in the culture that until then, she could admire only from afar. There, she heard Prokofiev for the first time, encountered the masterpieces of neoclassical painting, and next to the modern architecture of Düsseldorf, explored the Romanesque and Gothic churches whose style she admired. There, she immersed herself in the German poets she had read as a child, namely Hugo von Hofmannsthal, Stefan George, and Rainer Maria Rilke.[8] And it was there, far away from the insular community of her childhood, that she earned her PhD in Semitic languages and began to feel at home.

When she reached Palestine at the age of twenty-four, Goldberg was already known as a significant emerging poet in contemporary Hebrew literature, one of the first woman poets to be heralded by the predominantly male literary establishment.[9] Such was her status, and such was the state of Hebrew culture, that her arrival was marked by an announcement in one of the leading newspapers of the day. But the open arms that greeted Goldberg upon her arrival couldn't embrace her ambivalence.

Goldberg's Israel rests far from the biblical land of myrrh and frankincense, as well as from the nationalistic homeland that was frequently depicted by her contemporaries. In "And a Third Autumn," the parched starkness of the Mediterranean landscape, rather than its grandeur, pervades:

> Thistle. Bramble. Stones. I crossed
> over the rock. A bristling horizon,
> thistle without end—a land
> of brier and thorns,
> and strange birds coming to me.

The Hebrew's strongly stressed syllables, hard letters, and abrupt stops, which the translation seeks to mime—*Thi*stle. *Bram*ble. *Stones*. I *crossed* / *ov*er the *rock*. A *bris*tling horizon—animate Isaiah's admonition: "With arrows and with bows shall men come thither, because all the land shall be briers and thorns."[10] Crossing the barbed landscape, Goldberg gently diverges from almost an entire tradition wherein the land of Israel is nearly synonymous with home.[11] Are the birds "strange" because they are unknown to her, or because she is unknown to them? In "Pines," a poem from an earlier collection, Goldberg unravels the cliché of the exuberant bird-in-flight: "Maybe only the birds know / as they hang between earth and heaven / this pain / of two homelands."[12]

Perched between two disparate landscapes, Goldberg recoiled against what she referred to in her journal as the stream of "cultural fascism" that treated the study and translation of European literature as a threat to Hebrew literary culture.[13] She also diverged from her peers in the Yachdav poetic movement, Natan Alterman and Avraham Shlonsky, whose expectation that literature serve the Hebrew nation-building went against her grain. In fact, on the eve of World War II, in a heated polemic between herself and Alterman in the popular local newspaper, the twenty-eight-year-old Goldberg plainly held her ground: "Not only is the poet allowed to write love poems during a time of war, but rather, he *must*."[14]

Nor did Goldberg accept the homogenizing Zionist version of the melting pot, which expected that immigrants silently blend into their adopted culture. When Goldberg speaks for the collective, then, it is the fragile particulars that draw her attention. As her friend, the poet Tuvia Rübner, has said, "I have no talent for ideology, because it demands loyalty from its followers, and I'm capable of being loyal only to people. Not to ideas."[15] Goldberg shared similar fidelities. Take, for example, her rendering of the arrival of Jewish immigrants to Tel Aviv in the first section of her retrospective poem "The Shortest Journey":

The travelers' bags moved through the streets
and the language of a foreign land
was thrust like the cold blade of a knife
into the hot desert wind.

How did the air of that small city
find a way to bear so many

memories of childhood, lovers shed,
rooms emptied somewhere?

For these immigrants, a good number of them refugees from Nazi Europe, relocation bore the terrible weight of departure from language, from childhood places that would be lost forever, from old loves. It reduced them—as she suggests, literally as well as figuratively—to the bags they carried on their backs. In Goldberg's panorama of mass immigration, at the foreground stand those rooms, however empty, where people lived.

THE NIGHT IN THIS BOOK

"The night in this book is different: opaque, heavy—but maybe occasionally it still has something of the enchanting inanimate world which is in the title poem. I don't know," Goldberg wrote in a letter to Tuvia Rübner upon completing the manuscript of *With This Night*. Goldberg's self-effacing description of the collection intimates the alluvial mix of sorrow, wonder, and skepticism that courses through this volume and sets it apart from her earlier work. Though she was only fifty-three when she finished writing the poems of *With This Night* (first published in 1964), Goldberg's frail health made her feel much older than she actually was, and she seems to have been aware of her approaching death (which would come six years later). In "Looking at a Bee," this marriage of despair and awe is rendered with deceptive facility:

In the sunlight, she was a golden leaf falling,
in the blossom, a dark drop of honey,
in a swarm of stars, a bead of dew—
and here, she is shadow.

A single word in the whirring swarm,
urgent news in the lazy summer heat,
the play of light in twilight's dusty glow—
and here, she is shadow.

No light without the shadow—no insight without it, either. Quintessentially Goldbergian, each image, each idea, corresponds to the next, evoking a gentle, satisfying symmetry. Against the night stars, this bee-poet transforms into a bead of dew; in another swarm, she's a word; in the summer weather, a larger, more pervasive piece of language. The repetition of "here," which modulates the poem's rapid shifts, softens the landing of each stanza. Yet, the gratifying clarity of her lines notwithstanding, there's a good rule of thumb for reading Goldberg: if no ambivalence is to be found, read again. Without any explicit antecedent in the poem, "here" is gently self-referential, directed toward the language of the poem itself. The poet, who is inevitably "shadow"—amorphous, deflected, hidden from view—in her stanzas, finds a place to rest.

Poetry, the life of poetry, gave Goldberg a home, and yet, even while offering a place to dwell, it provided little shelter from the elements. Her previous collection, *Early and Late*, was subjected to criticism from younger critics who were looking for what they viewed to be a more open, less constricted poetics. With characteristic grace, in several poems of this collection she despairs, laughs, and defends her aesthetic—in response to their critique.[16] And though clearly she was influenced by the free verse revolution in Israel, most likely, something less affected and more effecting than mere acquiescence to fashion catapulted the breakthrough of *With This Night*. While writing the poems of this collection, Goldberg, who never married and had no children, frequently mentioned in her journal feelings of "suffocation." Her isolation during the late 1950s intensified with life-threatening pneumonia and chronic skin problems for which she was frequently hospitalized, and a final, devastating passion for a visiting lecturer in the Department of Comparative Literature at the Hebrew University during the early 1960s added to her sense of loneliness; this, like her earlier loves, was unrequited. Around the same time, Goldberg wrote in a letter to a friend that she was writing less frequently "not only because of exhaustion and stress, but also because as the years pass, I feel more and more responsibility toward the things I say."[17] Whatever the reasons were, rather than replicate the splendor and flash of her penultimate collection, here she gives glory to the dappled, the stippled, the spare and sometimes strange. Here is a collection she could lucidly describe by writing simply: "I don't know."

Abandoning many of the formal strictures of her earlier collections, in *With This Night*, Goldberg bends and blurs the meter and rhyme schemes that distinguished her earlier work, making room for a more exposed voice and music. In "From Songs of Two Autumns," Goldberg calls upon traditional Romantic figures—autumn, winter—for loss and transience, but as never before, she permits herself to leave statements unexplained, to experiment with diction and register, and to shatter syntax in the service of what seems like spontaneous utterance:

> Somewhere something someone there—
> a dark dawn, granite grazing the surface.
> The river, the leaves in the falling of their rustle,
> song of the grove.
> I'm passing—

Bearing out Eliot's conviction that "no verse is free for the man who wants to do a good job,"[18] Goldberg ruptures the metrically symmetrical lines that seemed to come so effortlessly for her. Compressing the knowledge of her approaching death into two words and the white space thereafter, "I'm passing—" Goldberg's lines ripple into darker, less certain, territory.

WHOLE AGAIN

"It is difficult / to get the news from poems," writes one of Goldberg's American contemporaries, "yet men die miserably every day / for lack / of what is found there."[19] In recent years, Israelis seem to have found, once more, something crucial in the work of Leah Goldberg. Her writing has received unprecedented attention over the past several years, with a volume of her complete journals, a collection of her short stories, critical editions of two novels, a volume of her correspondence, and a collection of her sonnets having appeared in print. In 2011 alone, a collection of her translations, a volume of her plays, and a gathering of her articles and public lectures are slated to appear. This is in addition to recent articles in newspapers, as well as new documentaries and performances based on her work and life.

What is it about Goldberg's voice that Israelis seem to need now more than ever? On the one hand, Goldberg experienced the events that shaped Israeli consciousness most irrevocably: like many of her generation, she grew up in the shadow of World War I, barely escaped Nazi Germany, and on Israeli soil, lived through the wars of 1948, 1956, and 1967. Yet, she had no interest in celebrating gallantry or hallowing the grief of survivors. In fact, her work brings a refreshing counter-beat to the often ideological sound bites of Israeli discourse. Counter, but not anti: it is directed against no particular government, no war, no establishment, no individual, aspiring toward neither protest nor resolution. In so doing, she realizes what her predecessor Haim Nahman Bialik deemed to be the function of poetry: a language that shines with newness, a fullness altogether other than the means-to-an-end utility of daily discourse.[20]

To what, then, did she aspire? "Art for art's sake" might come to mind. But for Goldberg, poetry was the "real world," the here and now, the shaping and reshaping of an essential, almost primordial sphere of values on which human life at each moment relies. Throughout her life, Goldberg witnessed the trampling of these values but continued to believe that the poet's task was to love the world nonetheless.[21] As she saw it, by crafting things of beauty, she was somehow capable, if only in some small way, of transforming the dread within and without. It is this particular quality of the Hebrew word *tikkun*—literally, "fixing," of oneself and one's world, in no way separable from language—that stands at the center of Goldberg's rigorous poetics. Her reflection in an interview shortly after her forty-eighth birthday bears out her conviction: "As a person ages, he experiences the reality of his era as belonging not only to him, but to all his generation. If he writes honestly, then in all that he writes this reality will necessarily find expression."[22]

In one of the lesser-known poems of *With This Night*, this reality finds expression when a wise man, a fool, and a dreamer gaze upon a pile of shards. In response to the scene, the wise man declares his righteousness, the fool remains oblivious, and the dreamer renders it complete even as he anticipates the next shattering:

But the dreamer wept, for he knew
two shards can never
be put back together:
each piece in his hands became
whole and then—
was broken again.

("Three Peered")

In this buried ars poetica, Goldberg, like the dreamer, anguishes over the world's brokenness, exacerbated by the boasting of the wise and the fools who close their eyes. Though she believed in no redemption, ideology or ideal that could set things right, she never ceased to seek wholeness, whether in the clarity of her line, the quality of her thought, or the dream of a more humane world. As she saw it, poetry made all this possible, and she demanded no less of herself. In her hands, a vision of the irreparable becomes—if only for a moment—whole again.

NOTES

1. From Goldberg's travel journal to Norway and Denmark, July–September 1960. The journal was found by Giddon Ticotsky at the Asher Barash ("Gnazim") Institute, Tel Aviv. (The journal is separate from the volume of Goldberg's complete journals published by Sifriat Poalim in 2005.)

2. Arieh Arad, "Yalduti beArei haLekhem" (Interview with Leah Goldberg), *BaMahaneh*, January 20, 1970.

3. Ibid.

4. Cf. "Songs of the Strange Woman."

5. Cf. Goldberg's largely autobiographical novel, *VeHu haOr* (Tel Aviv: Sifriat Poalim, 2005), 185.

6. Leah Goldberg, "I efshar likhtov im ayn haNoseh matzik lekha keHavaya pratit," HaShulhan haMeruba: Ha'im amda sifruteinu al dam haShoah vehaTekuma? ed. Geula Cohen, *Ma'ariv*, October 2, 1963.

7. Arieh Arad, "Yalduti beArei haLekhem" (Interview with Leah Goldberg), *BaMahaneh*, January 20, 1970.

8. Cf. Goldberg's childhood correspondence with her friend Minna Landau, where Goldberg's early interest in the works of European poets begins to blossom: *Nearot Ivriot: Mikhtavei Leah Goldberg min haProvintzia, 1923–1935*, eds. Giddon Ticotsky and Yfaat Weiss (Tel Aviv: Sifriat Poalim, 2009).

9. Goldberg hints at the tenuousness of her position as a woman in this literary culture in her well-known poem "Portrait of the Poet as an Old Man."

10. Isaiah 7:24 (King James Version).

11. With a few notable exceptions, e.g., certain poems by Yocheved Bat-Miriam, Esther Raab, and Shaul Tchernichovsky.

12. "Ilanot," *Barak baBoker* (Merhavia: Sifriat Poalim, 1955), 39.

13. Cf. Peter Cole, ed., *Hebrew Writers on Writing* (San Antonio: Trinity University Press, 2008), 139.

14. Leah Goldberg, "Al oto haNoseh atzmo," *HaShomer haTza'ir*, September 8, 1939.

15. Tuvia Rübner as quoted in Adina Hoffman, *My Happiness Bears No Relation to Happiness: A Poet's Life in the Palestinian Century* (New Haven: Yale University Press, 2009), 158.

16. Goldberg's ars poetica, "Portrait of the Poet as an Old Man" (particularly section 3), as well as "About Myself," "Lone Drum," and "New Spring, Old Version," explores the tension between these critics' expectations and her aesthetic predilections.

17. Leah Goldberg, letter to Fanny Pinnes, June 30, 1957, from the Asher Barash ("Gnazim") Institute, Tel Aviv.

18. "The Music of Poetry," *On Poetry and Poets* (London: Faber and Faber, 1969), 37.

19. William Carlos Williams, "Asphodel, That Greeny Flower," *Pictures from Brueghel* (New York: New Directions Books, 1962), 153.

20. Title essay in Haim Nahman Bialik, *Revealment and Concealment* (Jerusalem: Ibis Editions, 2000).

21. Cf. Goldberg's impassioned statement concerning the role of poetry in the world in "Al oto haNoseh atzmo," *HaShomer haTza'ir*, September 8, 1939.

22. A. B. Yoffe, "Bereishit ha'ita haMangina, bereishit ha'ita haRitmus: Sicha im Leah Goldberg," *Yediot Aharonot*, January 28, 1977 (originally printed in 1959).

WITH THIS NIGHT

Only from the graves of night, on my bed,
sometimes from afar I've seen
a black tree by starlight,
and my heart every now and then
remembered—at sunrise it is green.

WITH THIS NIGHT

With this night and all its silences
with this night—
with three stars
lost in the trees
with this wind.

With this wind
that stopped to listen
to this night—
with this night
and three stars
and this wind.

THE SHORTEST JOURNEY

1. Tel Aviv, 1935

The flagpoles on the roofs of homes
were like the masts of Columbus's ship
and each crow that perched on them
announced another continent.

The travelers' bags moved through the streets
and the language of a foreign land
was thrust like the cold blade of a knife
into the hot desert wind.

How did the air of that small city
find a way to bear so many
memories of childhood, lovers shed,
rooms emptied somewhere?

Like pictures blackening inside a camera,
clear winter nights were reversed,
and rainy summer nights across the sea,
and foggy mornings of capital cities.

As the marching behind your back
drums out a foreign army's songs,
it seems—as you turn your head to the sea,
your city's church is floating.

2. An Evening in a Café

The city's in the colored coat
of awnings over balconies,
clear wine shining in lanterns
and light in the drinks blurring.

Scraps of a squabble and a rush
of chatter, cutlery. High in the sky,
lights have erased from the blackboard
an old accounting of the stars.

The sea behind our backs,
short-tempered and severe,
tracks and charts our beating hearts
in a secret pact with my watch.

Only the very young can grasp
time's worth and meaning,
with its nights gone astray
and all that slips away
in each moment, vainly passing.

And like an incredible nightmare
there across the street,
an old man passes, slowly, surely:
he has no reason to hurry.

3. Rainy Autumn Night and a Clear Morning

Into a dark, opaque night
whose alleys
only the jackals know,
the city was thrown:

dressed in white,
unprotected
from lashes of rain,
the rebuke of thunder,
an old sea's stolen caress.

Our little city
together with us
and our lives—

but the bright morning opened her prison
and here—

black circles beneath her damp lashes—
she is white, and not fair
without a past or prideful air—
how beautiful was her youth!

4. She Still Had

She still had the scent of the sea,
of shells, orange peels, the warm wind of almost-summer,
and that magic of something uncertain—
known like a dream already dreamt.

Surrounded by water and light, a hundred ripples
held in her a taste of salt, longing—

my insatiable youth, my parched sands,
all the crowns of my sadness scorning the kingdom—
and the city, a white island on green waves.

5. Then I Walked Through the World

Then I walked through the world
as though someone adored me.
Laughter unfurled through heaps of stones,
and a wind through fathomless skies.

Then I walked through the world
as though someone dreamed me fair.
Across the night abysses bloomed
and the sea's mirror painted my face,
as though someone were writing poems about me.

I walked, until I reached an utter stillness within:
then, it seemed, something might begin.

6. The Shortest Journey

The shortest journey is across the years.
The light has not gone out. The house teeters,
a wall shifts. And here they stand
together like neighbors,
my night of now, my day of then.
What did they say: We're changing, aging?

The shortest journey is into the past.
Do you remember? A cool sea, two boats touching—
children on a hill have lifted a torch—
are we aging? Changing? Know this: until tomorrow,
such long hours are before me.

MY SUMMER RESORTS

1. There Still

Four sparrows
were singing
four springs
in a row.

And summer oozed
a stifling scent:
in the garden,
the tobacco
bloomed
four years
in a row.

That's over.
And there?
There the hammock still hangs in the breeze,
and a pinecone falls beneath the tree.
There isn't a single cemetery.
There's nothing left to see.
Today, no one is there
to say the Mourner's Prayer.

2. Almost Love

It's very simple:
wet grass,
a tree, and a bench.
That's all.

The canopy was full, a pine,
and the grass was wet with rain.
Three days have nearly passed
and we have yet to go out again.

—Of all evenings!
—Why not this one?
—The woods are drenched,
entirely.

We can't stay
on the bench any longer.
Let's go home,
and that is all.

How uncertain
and young he is,
the lights of a bicycle
on the way to town.

At home, the candles
make my pallor glow:
—hadn't I warned
that you'd catch cold!

3. The Neighbors Have Already Packed Their Bags

Someone came and said:
The Days of Awe are near.
Summer has passed.
And in the garden a pear
fell in the yellowing grass.

Someone came and said:
Summer ended fast.
And spring was shorter still.

At night the candle's shadow
stretched along the wall.
The neighbors have packed their bags.
We, too, soon will go.

In the city they're waiting
for us, and the Days of Awe.

OLD REFRAIN

Not even I was willing. And again
it rose in me like smoke,
devouring my eyes with its bitter fumes.
That same old tune!

I resisted. But my strength
failed me again:
my tracks led me
back to the cage.

And here I am,
just the same—
a foolish bird with bright colored feathers,
humming an old refrain
about what never was.

THE VANISHING NIGHT

The vanishing night, as if the roosters were crowing.
I am not able to rise.

The morning light. As if the doors were beating drums.
I am not able to rise.

The day will bend under the weight of this heat,
smothered by the oleander's sweet scent,
tongue withered in its bitter mouth.
And still I cannot open my eyes
and beat back with a glance
that which never ends.

SONGS OF THE STRANGE WOMAN

1.

I am green and fresh as a song through the grass,
I am deep and soft as the nest of a bird.
I'm from days long past,
from a forest, where I learned to breathe,
from the languor of lovers asleep in the grass.

I'm from there—
the village of small winds.
On a far hill there was a windmill,
and the sky hung on its wing
clouds mingled with smoke.
The wind comes and the wind goes.
I'm from the land that taps with wooden spoons
—from there.

2.

Windmill, O windmill,
on what shore did the gulls call
the name of my dead country?
Windmill, O windmill.

Along which street did the travelers pass,
sensing the sunset's kingdom
against their backs,
though they didn't turn their heads?
And the wings whirled in the wind.

Where
is the garden
red with autumn
that covered its shadows,
hid twilight in its leaves
and let the breeze pass through?

The wind called with the gull
the name of my dead country—
and here am I, silent and free,
windmill, O windmill!

3.

I was yours, land of low winds,
my heart carries each drop of your rain.
Stumbling, I'll bring—
no angel will help me—
mushrooms from your woods
to the kingdom of heaven.

In my kingdom of heaven,
they still remember your feast.
A cheerful harmonica plays the Song of the Dead.
One star is tangled in the windmill,
turning round, turning round—
but I'm already old and gray, and no one will dance with me.

Still, the gate is open, so I'll join the feast,
unlace my shoes and sit in the shade.
My face will gently flow down the faltering stream,

my face from the shore
of your river—
bright when I remember—
windmill, O windmill.

JOURNEY WITHOUT A NAME

1.

Where am I? How could I ever explain where?
My eyes are reflected in no window.
My face appears in no mirror,
and without me, all the city's streetcars pass.

Though the rain keeps falling, my hands are dry.
And here I am, all of me,
in a strange city,
in the heart of a vast homeland of strangeness.

2.

My room is so small
that the days lie low and grow careful,
and I too live cautiously within
the smell of smoke and apples.

At night, the neighbors will light a lamp:
beyond the large yard, past the birch's spreading branches,
a window across from me silently glows.
Sometimes at night it's hard to remember

that once, somewhere—
I had such a window.

3.

Weeks now, no one has called me
by name. It's simple:
the parrots in my pantry
have yet to learn it,
and no one in the city knows it.
And it exists only on paper, in writing,
and has no voice, no note, no ring.

For days I walk without a name
down a street whose name I know.
Without a name, I gaze for hours
at a tree whose name I know.
And sometimes, nameless, I wonder
about one whose name I do not know.

4.

I walked with the ships and stood with the bridges,
I was cast across the street
with the elm's falling leaves.
I had autumn, a cloud glowing
near a black chimney,
and a strange name
no one could guess.

Elul 5720, Copenhagen

SONGS OF FORGETTING

1.

My memory is clear as a spring
in which—everything shatters.
Your name and face are shards.

Your name and beautiful face:
how did they survive in a well?
Don't say:
In the well, they were whole
and now they're scattered in the wind.

They're scattered in the wind today,
they fall into the river's expanse,
and all rivers flow into the sea,
though the sea is never full.

2.

Someone tomorrow will turn to me and say:
Didn't we meet in Norway?
And in fact, a ship sailed
between the sun and moon.
I met there with a seagull,

a mountain made of lime,
and I think I saw on a certain street
a man with green eyes.

But you, sir, carry an umbrella,
and never venture outside,
and you were the jailer who kept me in
a land whose houses I've forgotten.

3.

Forgetfulness said: *It's impossible*
and since then, I've been at ease.
All the trees answer *Amen*
to the decaying leaves.

FROM THE *SYMPOSIUM*

Outside, the cats are wailing.
Yes, as always, my dear Aristophanes,
you never fail to amuse.
You've set the stage for ridicule:
all the pines, all the olives in the square,
answer my love with laughter.

And she, born to a god and a beggar,
dispossessed of house or inheritance,
will lie on the earth beneath a star.
She'll hear a nightingale in the cats' cry,

as the nearby sky grows wide.

DUST OF THE CROWN

1.

Yesterday on this little isle
a little evening reclined,
and gazed from the wondrous hidden distance,
until the gloom of night arrived
and swept the little island aside.
Listless people passing through were
sealed within the darkness too.

Around town, children played
with my fallen crown.

2.

The princess is old,
and the prince
spends the night in taverns.
The long road is white
with the glow of the moon's frost,
and the world is asleep,
except one barking dog.

3.

For you, half the kingdom . . .
since then, no one ever divined
the meaning of that dream
until a girl stood up and tried:
If he so loved Queen Esther,
why not the entire thing?

GAME OF DICE

Only toward the day's end did the moon descend.
Later, clouds built towers in the sky.
A lighthouse looks out over the waves,
ruling over the fish in the sea.
And we have sailed
far away.

Darkness fell among us—
a black die marked "one."
Within this black expanse, in memory, you wane.
At night, I have no luck. I lose the game.

THREE PEERED

Three peered at a pile of shards:
one was wise, one a fool, one a dreamer.
The wise man said:
I walk the straight and narrow path,
from a world without pity to a world without solace—
and I knew this was prophecy.

Nothing's happened to the whole,
the fool declared.
It only seems to be broken.
If only I weren't such a fool,
it might be repaired.

But the dreamer wept, for he knew
two shards can never
be put back together:
each piece in his hands became
whole and then—
was broken again.

LOOKING AT A BEE

1.

In the square light of the window—
on the pane, from outside,
a bee's shadow
so slight you can hardly see her wings.

She's on her back.
Narrow.
Six thin legs—
exposed
and bare,
an ugly threat,
the bee crawls.

How will we crown her in poetry?
What would you propose?
A little boy will come and announce:
The queen has no clothes.

2.

In the sunlight, she was a golden leaf falling,
in the blossom, a dark drop of honey,
in a swarm of stars, a bead of dew—
and here, she is shadow.

A single word in the whirring swarm,
urgent news in the lazy summer heat,
the play of light in twilight's dusty glow—
and here, she is shadow.

3.

And your honey?
Who will remember your honey?
It's over there, in the hive.
Here, on the lit pane, your head, your body—
all of you a stinger, helpless loathing, pitiful and blind.
The fear will kill you.
Beware.

FROM SONGS OF TWO AUTUMNS

1.

Somewhere something someone there—
a dark dawn, granite grazing the surface.
The river, the leaves in the falling of their rustle,
song of the grove.
I'm passing—

I'm passing like this autumn
setting its foot on the first ice:
stark, opaque, brittle, and falling
and buried in this dark, rainy dawn.

I pass like that star
slowly slipping into the not-quite-light
behind the horizon, oblivion,
where it will meet another night.

2.

I'm passing like this pain
leaving my body,
joy of departure
as from this pain
leaving my body.

I'm parting from myself
as from this autumn,
the dawn's dark swans
and the wings of its clouds.

I'm passing without sadness the borders of change.
Tomorrow
the snow will silence my life
on the beautiful path,
my body that ached,
the autumn,
the flight of my dark swans.

3.

Here, autumn is the cusp of spring
and the pine, an eternal candle.
Do not look upon my vanishing,
for the pine is an eternal candle.

In the vineyard the leaves fell,
along the slopes the squill bloomed.
Do not look upon my vanishing:
a black candle burns in the hills.

In the hills the stone has been chiseled.
The grass is soft as a flock of sheep.
Do not look upon my vanishing,
for the pine is an eternal candle.

AND A THIRD AUTUMN

1.

Thistle. Bramble. Stones. I crossed
over the rock. A bristling horizon,
thistle without end—a land
of brier and thorns,
and strange birds coming to me.

Strange birds—their sharp call
and summer's sting. A stony autumn,
the sky burning bright at the edges.
Still. The rain has yet to come.

In the thistle dark gold is concealed,
in the thistle strange birds call out,
in the thistle toward a bristling horizon,
weary days, like beggars, meander.

2.

Lifeless land and living heavens
a stone's breath and the wind's death
a wide space and ruins—

my insatiable youth—
what a wasted, trampled path!
What a chill our death prepares
in the future's hidden lair.

FOR SOMEONE WHO DOESN'T BELIEVE

1.

For someone who doesn't believe
it's hard to live this year—
the fields ask for a blessing,
the sea asks for faith,
and you—don't ask for a thing.

My heart sleeps
and I'm asleep.
Silence cleaves to my dream,
and my dead walk through my slumber
as though through an ancient fortress.
How will I wake
when my heart does not believe,
and you don't ask for a thing?

2.

You don't ask for a thing—
not for this tree which has stood
for ten years, like a sentinel,

nor for this path,
which ten years later
has reached my door,
nor the clear figure
in the lake of my slumber.

You don't ask for a thing—
ships pass
with wide open eyes
like the blind,
and the sea keeps a vow of silence.
A single bird
seeks to sever
the desert's repose.
And you—you don't ask for a thing.

3.

Only the hills have risen,
and the hyssop on the walls.
Tear my sleep from me—
try to make me rise.

A lone morning,
a morning without an echo,
hovers above me.
Let it lean over me,
let it grieve,
for the morning has returned—
the prodigal son!

Only the hills have risen.
I am asleep.
Morning presses against the pane,
and calls me
by name, and I don't answer.

THEY'VE FOUND ETERNAL LIFE

1.

They've found eternal life,
and it is their eternal life,
but my heart is devoured
by desire for this world:

to hunger in its hunger,
to be quenched by its thirst,
to grow in the sprouting
of its seed and root

to love it
and to scorn it,
but to live within
its fervor, and its fears.

2.

You walked among the dead
and there were many dead,
you sought a living soul—
there was no living soul.

The faces of the dead were free
of pain, free of worry,
and you will ask for just
one thing: the gift of suffering.

You'll remember me fondly
as it was I who brought you pain,
since for you, I remain
a living well of suffering.

But now I'm among the dead
and my face like theirs is quiet,
and my face like theirs is free
of pain, free of worry.

3.

A sentinel stands guard
at the holy gate
and no one from the castle
comes to greet me,

for inside the castle,
your good friends have gathered,
and there is no room left
for other beloved guests.

Even when you died,
someone else was there:
my name was never written
in the book of your kingdom.

4.

Ten years after you die,
I'll know it was true that I'd loved you,
or ten years after I die,
you'll know it's true: you've forgotten me.
These are a few of the things that have been said
about the Book of the Dead.

ONCE, GOD COMMANDED US

Once, God commanded us to stand firm
under the terrible Tree of Life.
And we waited, hope-stricken, through years of a black wind—
maybe the fruit would fall at our feet?
But nothing happened.

And when it was time to fathom everything hidden
between us and Him,
we saw boughs bending over and brown leaves shedding,
and the wind blew in gusts across our faces.

Then a voice said: Today, you are free.
That's all. And it is good.

So I walked alone toward the blade of cutting cold
just a few steps,
up to that streetlamp dying out
at the corner of the road.

PORTRAIT OF THE POET AS AN OLD MAN

1.

I sit at my desk
and boys play on my grave.
I finish my final poem—
they erase my memory and name.
And no one will know that I
am the morning bird—the lark:
they say I've always been that cricket,
chirping from a corner in the dark.

2.

Why won't you stop, you fool,
putting together cursed words?
Why won't you stop, you fool,
honing clipped lines of verse?

You're alone, the city's fallen
asleep, all is still.
Your poems arrive like an old woman
bearing tales of her loveliness,
in a dress that's out of style . . .

—But I have loved her all the while.

3.

Don't try to keep up with the times,
they don't need your kind.
The times are headed elsewhere
and you are not welcome there.

Don't try to keep up with the times,
they don't need your kind.
The times, they want to bury you,
and leave, for others, your share.

NEW SPRING, OLD VERSION

1.

A new spring, a new spring!
Everything's green and alive.
The bee is already bringing honey
from the flowers to her hive.

And the nightingales . . . (though they tell us,
there are no nightingales in our land).
Well, never mind: some other bird
in the bush is heard.

The poet is suddenly bold
enough to rhyme, as in the days of old.

2.

As if to prove that we've aged,
a melody from way back when
has, once again, slipped into our poem
with all the innocence of those days.

The old naïveté, that old desire
full of all the familiar fare,
for it's spring, as far as the eye can see—
and that's nothing new, for nature, or poetry.

3.

He walked across the water
light and calm, and left
no footprints along the water,
and so it was, for thousands of years.

Again, we try to find
his reflection in the water,
the mirror of miracles.
Peaks join in the skies,
crowning the highest mountains.

But we, on the shore,
smell the gasoline from a nearby street.

OPHELIA

1.

My love,
the silver curl
of my first autumn mist
my lover—
while I lie on the cold ground,
behind my head
two angels of evil
guard the tranquility of my soul.

I said: No.
I'll tear apart
my tranquility
I'll tear apart—

let both of us be
erased by the storm.

2.

Only not as a flower
across the water's surface,
and not as a garland of myrtle
across the water's surface

but as a stone
that fell
and sank

and my three circles
across the abyss—
myself
my love
and the curse.

TWO BALLADS OF THE ABANDONED MAIDEN

1.

When he left, my legs were still bare.
My braided hair was disheveled.
When he left, the raven crowed:
Where, young girl, did you go?

And now,
my breasts burn . . .
Mandrakes,
the scent of my hands.
The raven watches over me
and returns
without me.

The wildflowers
I trampled.
Lord, I confess
I was defiled.
I adored him,
and abhorred myself.
When he returned, the raven crowed:
Where, young girl, did you go?

2.

How doth she sit
solitary,
to conceal the shame
of her illicit joy,
to conceal rapture's tears—
do not turn back and repent.

—You're already far away,
and I have stayed nearby.
Your flame in me burns
and will not subside,
the mark of Cain love has inscribed—
I will not turn back and repent.

A blessing spoke
among the cursed:
she lay down
on the ground in the dark.
Bitter dreams reside
in the flesh's cry,
cold nights are sure
to arrive—
and I will not repent.

LONE DRUM

1.

A house. Sky. Vista.
A never-ending street.
A bent old olive tree
and the drum beat.

A friend I might meet.
(Should I greet him or retreat?)
A bent old olive tree
and the drum beat.

Do not touch or expose.
Someday someone will believe:
there was a bent old olive tree
and the drum beat.

Yes, isn't that how it was . . .
We won't call a witness.
A street. A vista. The chilling stillness—
and the drum beat.

2.

They loved me very much,
until I stepped onto the scaffold,
they loved me very much,
but I stepped onto the scaffold.

They didn't say a thing
the day I stepped onto the scaffold,
and that's the way it happened,
how I stepped onto the scaffold.

A lone drum, lone drum,
beating through the town,
a lone drum, lone drum,
to the end of the town.
A lone drum, lone drum,
rolling down the street.
It's time to bury the dead:
no one weeps.

I walked to the scaffold,
the trees kept quiet,
I walked to the scaffold,
the streams were silent.

I walked to the scaffold,
the streets said not a word,
I stepped onto the scaffold—
not a soul stirred.

A lone drum, lone drum
droning through the town.
A lone drum, lone drum
to the end of the town.
A lone drum, lone drum
rolling down the road.
It's time to bury the dead—
and there are no shrouds.

THE STONE THE BUILDERS REJECTED

1.

The stone the builders rejected
hasn't become the foundation.
When you account for all the years
you are, as then, small and forlorn.

Something on your face has changed,
something changed beneath the surface—
the years' final account
amounts to wisdom and concession.

The time has come for stones to be scattered,
but you have found no treasures.

2.

Tears, now, are rare,
and words are scarce.
It isn't so hard to give in,
it isn't so hard to face.

Mornings surprise me less,
the night-tempests have abated.
There aren't too many joys,
disappointments are overrated.

Two eyes peer from a hazy
mirror in grim realization.
Is this the work of wisdom,
or, could it be—tedium?

3.

No, each day tells you
in a sensible, clear light.
Listen to its voice,
try not to argue.

So many have died,
the chasm has widened,
and suddenly, fear and grief
aren't so hard to fathom.

But why bemoan
what has already happened?
Stones more firm by far
were kept from the foundation.

OUR BACKS ARE TO THE CYPRESS

Our backs are to the cypress. We hide
the mountains behind our houses
are ashamed to look up at the stars
and rush to the bustling streets
lest our hearts—get lost in the expanse.

And so we live
in closed rooms,
on streets restrained
by phone and telegraph lines,
far away from all we loved in our innocence—
bound by time, beyond us.

FAR AWAY

1. Even This Very Landscape

Even this very landscape
doesn't want to hear
the beautiful words
with which I've adorned it,
even this lovely tree
has silenced me, for fear
my tongue will slip.

I had similar names,
but your name is like stone,
I had names that echoed,
and yours rustles in the tree.
I had many names
the name of God I didn't utter
and now
I'll hold my tongue,
lest the echo answer.

2. And of All the Dead

Far, far away—
and no one asks anything of me.
The oath has been
retracted,
and the captive
hasn't come back.

Of all the dead
whose eyes looked to me
there wasn't one
who wanted my grief.

3. It Isn't the Sea

It isn't the sea that is between us,
it isn't the abyss that is between us,
it isn't time that is between us,
it's—the two of us between us.

4. Far Away

Far, far away
from it all—
from all the beautiful houses
on city streets outside,
from a fallen leaf
and the single word
that the sages inscribed.

Far, far away—
I walked with the ships
and stood with the bridges
I'm passing without sadness the borders of change.
My lover—
now, from that utterly
flawless day
I've always remembered.
Far from my eyes
that saw clouds, a world.

Within my body, where no answer is relinquished.
Within this light
that kills the other light
which hasn't yet been extinguished.

5. Answer

Don't lament a thing,
and don't covet anything.
By now you've surely seen
that what you mourn is already gone.

ABOUT MYSELF

1.

My time is engraved within my poems
like the years of a tree in its rings,
like the years of my life on my brow.

I have no hard words—
delusion's valves.
My pictures
are clear as the windows of a church,
through which
one can see
the light shifting in the sky
and how those I've loved,
like dead doves, fall.

2.

It's simple:
there was snow in one country,
and thistles in another,
and a star in a plane's window
at night
over many countries.

And the things came
and commanded me: *Sing.*
They said: *We are words*
so I surrendered and sang.

And more: there was a long bridge
and a streetlight beyond
and the man didn't approach.
I said: did not approach.

3.

This didn't have to be:
not when humiliated,
not when elevated,
not even in grief.

Since then, I made a pact
with things unheard.
There are paths toward buried dreams
beyond words.

4.

I never loved a city
for the good it brought me.
I never hated a city
for the pain it taught me.

Seven gates
to that glorious city
through which my memory
comes and goes,

as the wind blows.

COMPASSION DOESN'T APPLY

1.

I am not for myself,
for you are not with me.
And I have no tree
or leaf in the wind,
for I am not for me.

I have no words.
Even that small one, *no,*
is mine no more:
whom could I refuse?

2.

If I don't forget you,
my tongue will cleave to the roof of my mouth.
And if I don't sever your memory
from the heart of my nights,
my bones will never
sing their song again.

Dry pile of thorns in this desert:
whom will you warm
and what
will the flame burn down!

3.

The words were my youth,
and my years,
this stone on my mouth.
How will I move my lips?

All my hymns have been slaughtered.
All my words,
murdered.
Even the name of this stone on my mouth
I cannot utter.

4.

The years pass and even
more words
are forbidden.

The years pass and even
more feelings
are forbidden.

The years pass
and each day
the burden
of suppressing wisdom
weighs more heavily,

and compassion
doesn't apply to those
who are sentenced to silence.

TOWARD MYSELF

The years have made up my face
with the memory of loves,
and adorned my head with light, silver threads,
making me beautiful.

My eyes reflect
the landscapes,
and paths I've tread
have straightened my gait—
tired and radiant.

If you saw me today
nothing would remain
of the past you knew—
I walk toward myself
with the face you looked for in vain
when I walked toward you.

NOTES

Unless otherwise indicated, my translations reflect the final edition in which With This Night *was published (Leah Goldberg.* Shirim, *Tel Aviv: Sifriat Poalim, 1986).*

Biblical quotations reflect the new Jewish Publication Society of America Version or the King James Version.

THE SHORTEST JOURNEY

An Evening in a Café (p. 5)

"The city's in the colored coat": Goldberg likens the variegated aerial view of Tel Aviv to Joseph's coat of many colors (cf. Genesis 37:3, 23).

"In a secret pact with my watch": In a later publication of this collection, Goldberg changed *bivrit starim* to *bivrit stavit*—"In an autumnal pact [with my watch]." Out of prosodic concerns, I have opted for the earlier version.

Rainy Autumn Night and a Clear Morning (p. 6)

In Hebrew, all nouns are gendered, and the word for city (*ir*) is feminine. Goldberg follows out the implications of this grammatical assignment and evokes the city of Tel Aviv as a young woman, referring to it as "she." Throughout the sequence, the story of Tel Aviv is the story of Goldberg, who came to the city from Europe as a young woman.

"Dressed in white": The once-white buildings of Tel Aviv inspired people to call it "The White City." The Hebrew *tzhorim*, a pure, almost blinding white, also suggests the gown of a bride. In this associative field, the lashes of rain (*maglev hamatar*), thunder (*ra'am*), and old sea (*yam zaken*), which are all masculine nouns, ravage and defile her.

"She is white, and not fair": A reversal of "I am black, but comely" (Song of Songs 1:5).

Then I Walked Through the World (p. 8)

"Then I walked through the world": In Hebrew, the line reads *Ani halakhti az*. The word *az* (lit., "then") resonates back through the line and ripples down through the poem. I have chosen the phrase "walked through the world" with the hope of conveying the exuberant fullness of the Hebrew and the wistful way of walking described here, which is not only through a physical place, but also through a place in time.

MY SUMMER RESORTS (p. 10)

The title of the poem in Hebrew is "Keytanot Sheli." When Goldberg was young, the word *keytanot* would have recalled countryside vacation places in the Diaspora.

The Neighbors Have Already Packed Their Bags (p. 12)

"The Days of Awe": Literally, the phrase reads "terrible" or "dreadful" days. Here, however, Goldberg is also referring to the "Days of Awe" (Yamim Nora'im), the Jewish holidays of Rosh Hashanah and Yom Kippur, when Jews are called upon to make amends for the past year. These holidays fall during the beginning of autumn.

SONGS OF THE STRANGE WOMAN (p. 15)

In postbiblical Canaan, an *isha zara* (in contemporary Hebrew, *foreign* woman) was not merely from another place: she was *strange*, and most versions of the Bible in English have translated her as such. The title of the poem associates Goldberg with this isolated and vulnerable figure, who, like her, comes from outside the land of Israel (Proverbs 2:16 and 7:5).

Section 3 (p. 17)

"Turning round, turning round": The wind, the star, and the aging speaker take their cue from Ecclesiastes: "Southward blowing, / Turning northward, / Ever turning blows the wind; / On its rounds the wind returns" (Ecclesiastes 1:6).

JOURNEY WITHOUT A NAME (p. 18)

With few subsequent changes, all four sections of this poem were composed in Goldberg's travel journal to Scandinavia in 1960. (The journal, to date unpublished, was found by Giddon Ticotsky at the Asher Barash ("Gnazim") Institute.) In the journal, Goldberg reflects on what very well may be what she coins in the first section of the poem "a vast homeland of strangeness": "Yesterday at about this time, something unexplainable happened. Suddenly it seemed to me that right here, in this loneliness, *I found myself*" (Goldberg's emphasis).

Postscript (p. 21)

In an uncharacteristic move, Goldberg roots this poem of existential aloneness in a place and time. In the Jewish lunar calendar, Elul is the month that typically falls in September or October, preceding

81

Rosh Hashanah and Yom Kippur. The notation 5720 is the Jewish year beginning from creation and corresponds to 1960.

SONGS OF FORGETTING (p. 22)

"And all rivers flow into the sea, / though the sea is never full" (Ecclesiastes 1:7).

FROM THE *SYMPOSIUM* (p. 25)

In the *Symposium*, Plato depicts a drinking party during which Socrates, Aristophanes, and others discuss the nature of love. At the feast, Aristophanes (448–380 BCE) offers a characteristically satirical account.

DUST OF THE CROWN

Section 3 (p. 28)

"For you, half the kingdom": "'What troubles you, Queen Esther?' the king asked her. 'And what is your request? Even to half the kingdom, it shall be granted you'" (Esther 5:3). See also Esther 5:6 and 7:2.

FROM SONGS OF TWO AUTUMNS

Section 3 (p. 36)

"Do not look upon": The archaic phrase *Al tiruni* appears just once in the Bible: "Look not upon me, because I am black" (Song of Songs 1:6).

AND A THIRD AUTUMN (p. 37)

"A land / of brier and thorns": Replete with all the Goldbergian ambivalence, these lines from Isaiah 7:24 are directed at the land of Israel: "With arrows and with bows shall men come thither, because all the land shall become briers and thorns."

"Still.": Goldberg stretches the conventions of Hebrew grammar in order to achieve the playful, sharply accented noun sequence *zeh stáv sharáv* (which probably means, "This is an autumn heat wave"). Here, I've taken liberty with the literal and have chosen to suggest the weight of those accents, and of the unseasonal Mediterranean heat, with a single-word sentence, "Still."

FOR SOMEONE WHO DOESN'T BELIEVE (p. 39)

Four decades before she composed this poem, then sixteen-year-old Goldberg reflected in her journal, "Today in class he said: 'Anyway, science cannot prove that God does not exist.' His face shone with delight. And so, he believes! How nice it must be for him: he has his God, and doesn't need to search. And how nice it must also be to believe there is no God, and to have no need for one. As for myself, I know nothing. I'm not at peace with this. I need some kind of faith. Without it, I won't be able to live" (December 8, 1927).

Section 1 (p. 39)

"My heart sleeps / and I'm asleep": Cf. "I was asleep, / But my heart was wakeful" (Song of Songs 5:2). Contrary to the biblical rendering, the speaker of Goldberg's poem is not woken.

Section 3 (p. 41)

"And the hyssop on the walls": Cf. I Kings 5:13.

"For the morning has returned— / the prodigal son!": Presumably an ironic exclamation of surprise, even disbelief, that the natural process of night becoming day has occurred.

"Morning presses against the pane, / and calls me / by name, and I don't answer": Weaving the biblical allegory into her own, Goldberg associates the dawn with the beloved in Song of Songs: "Hark, my beloved knocks! / 'Let me in, my own, / My darling, my faultless dove!'" (5:2).

THEY'VE FOUND ETERNAL LIFE (p. 42)

"My heart is devoured / by desire": Cf. Deuteronomy 32:24.

ONCE, GOD COMMANDED US (p. 46)

The Hebrew includes an epigraph: *In memory of Nadia,* a friend of Goldberg's who passed away at a young age.

"The terrible Tree of Life": Cf. Genesis 3:22–23.

"That's all. And it is good": Goldberg's colloquial *vezeh tov* (lit., "and this is good") echoes the biblical *ki tov*—"that it was good." (Cf. Genesis 1:4, 10, 12, 18, 21, 24.)

"The blade of cutting cold": The "fiery ever-turning sword" stationed east of the Garden of Eden guarded the way to the Tree of Life (Genesis 3:24).

PORTRAIT OF THE POET AS AN OLD MAN

Section 3 (p. 49)

"Don't try to keep up with the times": When asked, Goldberg refuted the suggestion that the poem contains a critique of Israel's then-new generation of free-verse poets: "I wanted to say that a poet shouldn't try to follow the fashion of the day simply because it is fashionable. I have my own means of expression and if it changes, it is not because of what's in style" (Interview with Ruth Bondy, "Ayn li milim kashot," in *Davar*, Oct. 30, 1964).

OPHELIA

Section 2 (p. 54)

"Garland of myrtle" recalls, of course, the bouquet Ophelia held when she drowned in the river, as recounted by Queen Gertrude: "There with fantastic garlands did she come / Of crow-flowers, nettles, daisies, and long purples" (*Hamlet* act 4, scene 7).

TWO BALLADS OF THE ABANDONED MAIDEN

Section 1 (p. 55)

"Where, young girl, did you go?": The Hebrew, "Na'arah, Na'arah!"—with the guttural *r* rolling into the open *ah*, onomatopoetic in this instance—*sounds* like a crow calling. In an effort to make this effect audible, I have deviated from the word-for-word rendering, "Young girl, young girl!," and have opted for phrasing that would in some measure replicate the linkage that Goldberg achieves between sound and sense in the Hebrew.

Section 2 (p. 56)

"How doth she sit / solitary": From the opening of Lamentations, which describes the desolation of Jerusalem after the destruction of the First Temple. A feminine noun in Hebrew, the city of Jerusalem doubles as a figure for the abandoned woman.

"Do not turn back and repent": The two words that comprise the Hebrew idiom for repentance, *lachzor bitshuva,* mean "return." The phrasing I have chosen aims to encompass those resonances in the English.

"The mark of Cain": Cf. Genesis 4:15.

THE STONE THE BUILDERS REJECTED

Section 1 (p. 60)

"The stone the builders rejected / hasn't become the foundation": Overturning the line from Psalms 118:22, *Even ma'asu habonim ha'ita lerosh pina* (The stone that the builders rejected / has become the chief cornerstone), Goldberg reappropriates the biblical slogan that had been used in the early years of the State of Israel, which promised triumph and redemption. This language is repeated in the third section of the poem as well ("Stones more firm by far / were kept from the foundation").

In an effort to retain the gently modulated music of the Hebrew, I have substituted the more common translation of *rosh pina*, "chief cornerstone," with "the foundation."

"The time has come for stones to be scattered": The Hebrew approximates Ecclesiastes 3:5: "A time to cast away stones, and a time to gather stones together."

FAR AWAY

Even This Very Landscape (p. 64)

"For fear / my tongue will slip" and "I'll hold my tongue": The Hebrew phrases, *pen echta besfatai* and *lo echta besfatai*, respectively, echo Job's first response to the tragedies he incurred: despite his wife's urging to curse God, he refused to "sin with his lips" (Job 2:10).

It Isn't the Sea (p. 66)

"It isn't the sea that is between us": Cf. "The Sea Between Us" ("HaYam beini uVeinkha"), by the major medieval Hebrew poet of Islamic Spain, Shmuel HaNagid.

Far Away (p. 67)

In a coda of sorts, Goldberg incorporates these lines from the following poems of this collection:

"I walked with the ships and stood with the bridges" ("Journey Without a Name").

"I'm passing without sadness the borders of change" ("From Songs of Two Autumns").

"My lover—" ("Ophelia").

Section 1 (p. 73)

"I am not for myself, / for you are not with me": Goldberg plays on the famous statement by Hillel the Elder, "If I am not for myself, who will be for me, and if I am only for myself, what am I, and if not now, when?" (*Ethics of the Fathers* 1:14).

Section 2 (p. 74)

"If I don't forget you, / my tongue will cleave to the roof of my mouth": A reverberation from Psalms 137:5–6: "If I forget thee, O Jerusalem . . . let my tongue cleave to the roof of my mouth."

"My bones will never / sing their song again": Literally, "My bones will never *say* a song again" (italics mine). Cf. Psalms 35:10: "All my bones shall say / 'Lord, who is like You? / You save the poor from one stronger than he, / the poor and needy from his despoiler.'"

Section 3 (p. 75)

"This stone on my mouth": A stone may also cover a well. Cf. Genesis 29:2.